FAIR IS OUR LAND

O I see flashing that this America is only you and me,
Its power, weapons, testimony, are you and me,
Its crimes, lies, thefts, defections, are you and me . . .
Freedom, language, poems, employments, are you and me,
Past, present, future, are you and me . . .

I am for those that have never been master'd,
For men and women whose tempers have never been master'd
For those whom laws, theories, conventions, can never master.
I am for those who walk abreast with the whole earth,
Who inaugurate one to inaugurate all . . .

(Democracy, while weapons were everywhere aim'd at your breast,
I saw you serenely giving birth to immortal children, saw in dreams
  your dilating form,
Saw you with spreading mantle covering the world.)

WALT WHITMAN: *By Blue Ontario's Shores*

FAIR IS OUR LAND

Designed and Edited by
SAMUEL CHAMBERLAIN
Introduction by DONALD MOFFAT

HASTINGS HOUSE, *Publishers*   NEW YORK CITY

A BUCKS COUNTY FARMHOUSE   *Wood Engraving by Thomas W. Nason*

Introduction

PATRIOTISM, like other kinds of love, finds its true nourish-
ment in the still places of the soul, in the hidden chambers
of the heart, not in our mouths. We Americans had slipped
into the easy habit of assuming that ours was the richest, therefore
the greatest, land on earth, powerful beyond fear of challenge;
and we said so, too loudly and too often.

Now to the ultimate good of our souls we are learning the truth:
that freedom and security cannot be bought on twelve easy pay-
ments. We are learning again a thing which our fathers well knew,
and which in our fatness we had forgotten: that love, whether it be
love of God, man, or country, grows by giving, not taking. We
dreamed of a heaven brought down to earth by closing our eyes and
wishing. No more! Heaven is there; but it may not be had for
nothing. Now we know that the earth is round, and our bit of it
subject to the same ancient laws that govern the rest. We had one

chance in 1919. We turned our backs, refused to shoulder our share of the burden, and plunged blindly into man's favorite sport, getting and spending.

Now the bill is rendered. For the first time in our history we are suffering shock. We have been wrong—colossally wrong!—and hurt in our tenderest spot, our pride. A load as heavy as Atlas's has been thrust upon us, suddenly, the way such burdens usually fall, and this despite the clearest of warnings. Today we face reality; we are entering upon the arduous task of proving that we are worthy of our destiny.

No man but has sometimes darkly wondered whether his secret faith were justified,—so easily may the little near blot out the distant great. In recent years a deafening babble has been dinning at our ears, striking doubt and despair in all but the strongest hearts. The voices have come hurling at us from all directions: the shriek of headlines pitched to shock us into buying two cents worth of vicarious sensation; the oily voice of radio, selling scented optimism and patriotism by the tube; the jingo's boastful shout, the warning croak of myopic little men called isolationists; the suave tones of government and the empty rumble of powerful interests; the defiant clamor of labor; the voice of Youth, cruelly mistaught to demand its "rights" to something for nothing; the crabbed voice of Age, begging sanctuary; and for a background the sound of money changing hands, the daily announcements of grandiose appropriations of money, which in our native fashion we take not for promise but for deed.

Listening to the loud claims and easy promises, it was easy to lose sight of the country's innate capacity for good sense and good will, and to forget how sadly the public accents were mistaken for the private voice of America. For this true voice is not a demanding one. Rather it is on the quiet side: low-pitched, a little wistful, inarticulate, prone to the expression of humorous doubts, and in reply to almost any kind of question, giving out the familiar "Guess so!" There is no lack of self-confidence in this homespun answer, merely a native attitude of cautious skepticism towards the ends of limbs: Guess so; reckon so; feller can always give it a try. It is as unlike British understatement as it is different from French irony or German rodomontade: a modest voice, often impatient, but naturally good-humored; a voice that goes well with the American face with its pale complexion and turned down lips and steady eyes. Sharpen your ears and listen. You will hear it, clear above and below and through the tumult: the voice of the little people from city and farm and shore, office, shop, and highway, the folk of many tongues and many customs who make up the great bulk of the free American people: the people who live in the land pictured in this book. Fine little people, utterly confident of becoming bigger and better and finer still. Listening, weighing, shrewdly judging, they have quietly moved out far ahead of their leaders, prepared their souls for the inevitable day of sacrifice. They are passing through the kind of unconscious metamorphosis which creates new races, which is now creating the American race, and which God willing may one day change us into citizens of a free world.

Was there ever such a land of paradox under the sun? Here we are, a hundred and thirty-odd million of us, living blithely on the assumption that each of us has a *right* to freedom, bread, and knowledge. We know that liberty may be had only through self-government: yet we have turned government over to a class of professionals who live by it, while we, poor sleepy fools, wake up only in time for the quadrennial debauch we call Election Day. We claim the right to bread,—the right to make, in the old homely phrase, a daily living: yet we have fallen into the sinful habit of thinking of this right not in terms of work, but of "jobs,"—a very different concept. We longed for knowledge, and set up the vast machinery of universal education,—surely the noblest dream of all. Yet we forgot to teach the gospel of personal responsibility, and so neglected Knowledge itself that we utterly failed to understand the lessons of this war, till suddenly it was upon us. We came into our great inheritance of natural wealth and wasted it on a scale more lavish than the imagination can grasp. The stuff was everywhere, on the ground and under it, for the taking. We took more than we could use, and spoiled more than we took, with never a thought for the generations to follow. The miracle is that somehow we still managed to cling to the principles of liberty, including the liberty to make fools of ourselves; kept them without giving up the price in blood that the older nations have had to pay periodically through all their histories.

Even in little ways we live by paradox. Consider our proudest possession, the automobile—sleek, silent, gleaming, powerful: we give it the speed of light, man it with twenty million itching toes, then are shocked to hear that this meteoric boudoir has slaughtered more than forty thousand of us in a single year,—more of us than were killed in action in the last war. In the West we plant mile after mile of shining wheat fields, enough to feed the world: then turn this treasure into a white insipid fluff that to our shame we give the honored title bread. We have even cleverly learned to put back into it by artificial means the vital germ the bread factories destroyed in the making. We call it bread, not pulp—a name reserved for our favorite reading matter, for the sake of which we have butchered our forests and laid bare the land on a scale to upset the very balance of Nature. We are at once the cleanest and the dirtiest of peoples. We make and sell enough different kinds of soapy cakes and powders and liquids to make us and our dwellings shine like new silver. Yet outdoors, in our yards and city streets and along our roads, we wade along through a slough of dismal trash. Push open the doors of the nearest corner drugstore, most characteristic of American institutions—market-place, amusement area, and social center rolled into one: along one wall the glittering counter pours forth a flood of icy syrups guaranteed to wreck the health of all but the toughest; and in glass cases across the way, shelf after shelf of antidotes guaranteed to make us well again. We take pride in the towering white miracles of our great cities and, in the name of democracy, turn them over to little gangs of grafters to run. We are chronically indifferent to preventing accidents; yet, if a catastrophe is shocking enough, no hearts are more quickly touched to charity. We enact more laws in a month than most governments do in a generation: yet crime has been one of our great industries.

Though our sins are many and heavy upon us, it may be truly said that they are the sins of youth which, like the gaucheries of any coltish boy, will doubtless be cured by time. Our self-consciousness, our sentimentality, our aversion to moderation if an extreme can be found to go to, our sudden violences and quick repentings—all are signs of immaturity, characteristics of a youth spoiled with a surfeit of good things too easily come by. So with our childlike faith in the magic of words, slogans, rather than in the ends they symbolize: Publicity, Service, Reform, Modern (and its little sister Streamlined), Safety First, One Hundred Per Cent, Automatic, Functional,—the list is endless. "Success" is our Holy Grail, even more potent as a vision than as an achievement. "Turnover," another wishing-ring, announces universal happiness in terms of Things, and the rapid production and consumption thereof: we have an unquestioning belief that the highest aim of man is to keep money whirling ever faster and faster in an ever greater eddy. One by one we take such patent panaceas for our ills, one by one they turn stale in the bottle and we hopefully open a new and more active vermifuge or prophylactic.

Like children we believe in the theory of the Royal Road, destiny's magic blue print. We know it exists—if only we could lay our hands on it!—and our pet divining-rod is a new law. Unlike the British, to whom law is the codification of tried and tested custom, we codify our hopes, enact our aspirations: first cut our legal coat, then try to force the body politic to fit it. Thus we gain a pleasing statutory Utopia which seldom works but which comforts our moral sense. It also conveniently helps us to forget that no Utopia worth having may be had for nothing. Actually, as every adult knows, there is no such thing as Utopia, except in terms of the struggle to achieve it. That is why in times of peace we long for the equivalent of the spirit that animates us in time of war: the sense of dedication to a whole that is dearer than any of its parts. Our reliance on statutory law has a charming, childlike quality, harmless enough—till we make the mistake of thinking of it as a substitute for true social progress: the slow, patient, precarious kind which alone is strong enough to survive the inevitable nine steps backward for every ten steps gained.

Nor, alas, is law a proper substitute for social responsibility, a sense in which we Americans are sadly deficient. No doubt we have plenty of excuses: the proud and holy debauch of materialism we've been indulging in for generations hasn't given us time to develop such responsibilities. We've been too busy: watching the wheels go round, opening the land, digesting the contents of the melting-pot, educating ourselves by the million, planting and reaping, building and tearing down and rebuilding our cities and factories, turning luxuries into necessities, making money and blowing it. Social responsibility is a thing we've never, in sheer self-defense, *had* to learn in order to survive.

We have loved our country with the careless love of youth. But we have loved it greatly. Now the honeymoon is over. Our foreign relations have moved in to stay, and the holy bonds of unity are changing from rhetoric to fact. For the first time in our history as a great nation our lives, not merely our property, are directly threatened. This is the kind of challenge we are fit to meet. For with all our faults we have certain virtues which in all humility we may claim as peculiarly American.

They are qualities which, used to the hilt, will eventually gain us a narrow victory over our enemies, and may some day help us build a civilization to match our dreams. Our poets salute the glory of their country as it is,—and much is revealed to them that is hidden from the ordinary mortal. Yet, truly, do they not sing rather of tomorrow's hopes than of today's achievements? We may be all their inspiration reveals: but when their dreams come true, will not the miracle prove to have been one of faith and courage alone?

For this is the great American virtue, this the American Dream: faith in our mastery of the future. This, with our passionate love of country, is what gives us courage to face the dark night with a lifting heart. We have not yet begun to understand how bitterly, how cruelly, it is to be tested in the years to come, nor glimpsed the immensity of the sacrifice the future will demand. But our faith will not betray us. We are free in fact. We are free from the clinging hand of tradition, in love with new ideas, new methods, fresh techniques; we are resourceful; we have a native ingenuity which helps us to adjust ourselves rapidly to new conditions; and for all our wastefulness and inefficiency, we have a tenacious and healthy determination never to quit a job till it is done.

We are free, and we are equal,—all of us. If this little word means anything, it means that in every smallest corner of the land there is a man ready to meet his duty and his opportunity, and to fill the place of the irreplaceable man above him. We have no peasant class, with its stout virtues and limitations. (Our migratory farm labor poses a different and more tragic problem which, with many another just as grave, awaits solution after the war.) We have no servant class, nor any master stock. We have only a free people able as individuals to greet the unforeseen, and deal with it in the way of free man. That is equality.

Faith is our talisman; it has many facets. Of them all the one that shines with the steadiest light is human friendliness. The pictures in this book show the grandeur and beauty of our country. In many of them you will see a human figure—no legendary Paul Bunyan, Pecos Bill, or John Henry, but a simple American. A sheepherder leans on his stick, the prairie sweeping away before him; a roadside shopkeeper peddles the great native staples—five gallons of gas and a hot-dog; a tourist sits on a log in the shade of a mighty stand of Sequoias; here a Vermont farmhand sweats on his sun-drenched hillside farm, and there a mountain man rests on the roof of the world to swing his eye over the savage white convulsion of the Rocky Mountains: wherever you find him, you, a perfect stranger, will find him simple, friendly, original and, if you don't make a fool of yourself, ready to go out of his way to do you a favor—or even have you in to meet the folks. He can afford to be hospitable: he is a free man, therefore unafraid. Though he may lack the peasant's fierce love of his land—he's too much of a migratory critter for that—he is his own master: where he pitches his shack he's the boss, and you, the man passing through, are his friend.

There's a new look in his eye today, and a new feeling in his heart. He is learning to see his country as a whole, beginning to understand the size of the job ahead of him, and buckling down to it. He's got what it takes and he knows it. Give him the tools and the weapons, and a little common sense up top, and there's nothing he won't gladly tackle and stick to till it's over.

All men are brave. Our generation of the world is perhaps the first to learn that courage is the commonest human virtue. All lands are fair. But the matchless beauty of our own land we now see in a new and clearer light; now, when we are learning to forget ourselves and fight to keep this beauty undefiled.

DONALD MOFFAT

WINDSWEPT   *Wood Engraving by Thomas W. Nason*

Contents

	PAGE
INTRODUCTION	9
EDITOR'S NOTE	21
TOWNS AND VILLAGES	25
INLAND WATERS	39
THE FARM	59
THE COUNTRYSIDE IN THE EAST AND SOUTH	85
THE GREAT WEST	117
OUR ARCHITECTURAL INHERITANCE	153
MOUNTAIN RANGES AND THE NATION'S PARKS	179
THE SEA COASTS	207
LIST OF ILLUSTRATIONS	241

BERKSHIRE HILLS   *Wood Engraving by Thomas W. Nason*

Editor's Note

THIS VOLUME seeks to portray the beauty of the American countryside, at a time when the preservation of this fair land, and all that it stands for, is uppermost in the minds of all Americans. It is the picture of a peaceful America, the land that awaits the returning soldier and sailor, serene and comforting. It does not encompass the might of our cities nor the dynamic energy of our industry. That is a theme for a book in itself. Above all, it is not a state-by-state encyclopedia of scenic wonders. Its objective is to distill the essence of rural America. The work of more than eighty etchers and photographers has been selected to give an unforgettable *impression* of this bright land. Their eloquent pictures speak for themselves, without the need of an interlocutor.

Many schools of thought are represented by these eighty artists. Among the etchers are both moderns and conservatives. The photographers are widely diversified. There are abstractionists, pictorialists, salon exhibitors and architectural specialists among them. Each makes a distinct contribution to the composite portrait of our homeland. To each I beg to express the keenest thanks and appreciation. I am grateful to the Library of Congress, the New York Public Library, Kennedy & Company, New York, and Goodspeed's Book Shop, Boston, for supplying the etchings for these reproductions. Finally, may I pay particular tribute to the assistance offered by the Farm Security Administration, the United States Forest Service and the United States Department of the Interior, all in Washington.

Here, then, is *your* America, a matchlessly fair land and a brave one— a land worth fighting for!

SAMUEL CHAMBERLAIN

BLACKSMITH'S SHOP   *Thomas W. Nason*

FAIR IS OUR LAND

Pownal, Vermont   *Gustav Anderson*

Towns and Villages

Midwinter – West Hartford, Vermont *Marion Post Wolcott for F.S.A.*

Wooden Gothic – Lancaster, New Hampshire *Rothstein for F.S.A.*

The Frary House – Old Deerfield, Massachusetts   *Samuel Chamberlain*

Berkshire Night   *Etching by Kerr Eby*

Summer Street

Drypoint by Samuel Chamberlain

FAIR IS OUR LAND

Bend in the Road – Newcastle, New Hampshire   *Drypoint by Samuel Chamberlain*

Springtime in the Village – Peterburg, New York   *Keystone*

TOWNS AND VILLAGES

Northernmost New England – Fort Kent, Maine   *Delano for F.S.A.*

New England Night   *Lithograph by C. W. Anderson*

FAIR IS OUR LAND

Cornwall Bridge   *Etching by Armin Landeck*

Easthampton, Long Island   *Tet Borsig*

TOWNS AND VILLAGES

Porch Light – Pierre, South Dakota   *Vachon for F.S.A.*

Main Street – Grundy Center, Iowa   *Rothstein for F.S.A.*

FAIR IS OUR LAND

Mrs. Ellis' Store – Falmouth, Virginia   *Frances Benjamin Johnston*

Prairie Village – Surrey, North Dakota   *Vachon for F.S.A.*

Tank Town – Bridgeport, Wisconsin   *Vachon for F.S.A.*

Colorado Hill Town – Ouray

Rothstein for F.S.A.

TOWNS AND VILLAGES

Ghost Town – Eureka, Colorado   *Lee for F.S.A.*

Silverton, Colorado   *Lee for F.S.A.*

FAIR IS OUR LAND

Silver Peak, Nevada   *Rothstein for F.S.A.*

Pre-historic Village – Mesa Verde   *Cedric Wright*

Montana Prairie Town   *Rothstein for F.S.A.*

Pueblo Village – Taos, New Mexico   *Rothstein for F.S.A.*

FAIR IS OUR LAND

Hinckley Lake – Ohio

Ewing Galloway

Inland Waters

Lake in the Hills – North Carolina

Ewing Galloway

FAIR IS OUR LAND

Sunset on Newfound Lake – New Hampshire   *Arthur Hammond*

Sand Dunes on Lake Michigan   *Underwood and Underwood*

INLAND WATERS

Trapper's Lake – Colorado   *U. S. Forest Service*

Lake Tarryall   *Lithograph by Adolph Dehn*

Tilden Lake – Yosemite National Park   *Cedric Wright*

Klamath Lake – Oregon   *Ray Atkeson*

Spirit Lake and Mt. St. Helens   *Ray Atkeson*

Gold Mill – Colorado   *Lee for F.S.A.*

San Carlos Lake – Arizona   *Josef Muench*

St. Mary's Lake – Glacier National Park   *U. S. Dept. of the Interior*

Seven Lakes Basin – Olympic National Park   *Asahel Curtis for U. S. Dept. of the Int.*

Crater Lake – Oregon   *Ray Atkeson*

Lost Lake – Oregon   *Ray Atkeson*

INLAND WATERS

Trick Falls – Glacier National Park

Hileman

FAIR IS OUR LAND

Niagara Falls
Ewing Galloway

The Dam at Pigeon Forge – Tennessee
Ewing Galloway

INLAND WATERS

Punch Bowl Falls – Oregon
C. M. Ballard for U. S. Forest Service

Swift Current Falls – Montana
Hileman for Glacier National Park

FAIR IS OUR LAND

Glen Aulin Falls – California — *Cedric Wright*

River Bend in Provo Canyon – Utah — *Ray Atkeson*

The York River – Maine   *Etching by R. Stephens Wright*

Curiosity   *Etching by Frank Besedick*

The Sweeping Ohio   *B. W. Muir for U. S. Forest Service*

Steamboat on the Kentucky River   *Ewing Galloway*

West Point *Etching by Gerald K. Geerlings*

Mississippi Evening *Etching by Otto Kuhler*

The Amy Hewes – Louisiana   *Ewing Galloway*

Mississippi River Ferry – Helena, Arkansas   *Arkansas State Publicity Department*

The Colorado River   *Hubert A. Lowman*

North Platte River – Nebraska   *Underwood and Underwood*

High Water on the Sacremento River

Grant Duggins

INLAND WATERS

The Columbia River Gorge   *Ray Atkeson*

Indian Salmon Fishermen – Columbia River   *Ray Atkeson*

FAIR IS OUR LAND

The Grande Ronde Valley – Oregon   *Minor White*

The Farm

A Pennsylvania Landscape *Woodcut by Thomas Nason*

Farm on the River *Drypoint by Chauncey E. Ryder*

FAIR IS OUR LAND

August Afternoon on the Farm — Rowley, Massachusetts   *Samuel Chamberlain*

Hilltop   *Eleanor Park Custis*

Barns in Winter – Putney, Vermont   *Marion Post Wolcott for F.S.A.*

The Casey Farm – North Kingston, Rhode Island   *Samuel Chamberlain*

Abandoned Farm – Hampton Falls, New Hampshire   *Samuel Chamberlain*

Hay Cutting Time in Vermont   *Rothstein for the F.S.A.*

New England Farm on the Merrimac

Eleanor Park Custis

FAIR IS OUR LAND

Pennsylvania Farmland   *Marion Post Wolcott for F.S.A.*

Harvest in Ohio   *Ewing Galloway*

Farm on the Atlantic Shore   *Samuel Chamberlain*

Barns of Purissima   *C. Stanton Loeber*

String Bean Pickers – Cambridge, Maryland   *Rothstein for F.S.A.*

Barn With Stone Silos – Maryland   *Henry Flannery*

THE FARM

Log Farm House – Roanoke, Virginia   *Frances Benjamin Johnston*

Old Slave Quarters – Eastville, Virginia   *Frances Benjamin Johnston*

Upland Farms of Virginia – Autumn Near Marion.   *Marion Wolcott for F.S.A.*

Upland Farms of Virginia – Winter – Rappahannock County *Rothstein for F.S.A.*

Tobacco Field in the Kentucky Mountains   *Marion Post Wolcott for F.S.A.*

Tobacco Harvest   *Marion Post Wolcott for F.S.A.*

Contrasting Farms in Kentucky – The Backwoods   *Marion Post Wolcott for F.S.A.*

Dairy Farm in Jefferson County – Kentucky   *Marion Post Wolcott for F.S.A.*

THE FARM

Mississippi Mule Team   *Marion Post Wolcott for F.S.A.*

Cotton Picking Time – Benoit, Mississippi   *Marion Post Wolcott for F.S.A.*

The Fertile Earth   *Lithograph by Albert W. Barker*

Footbridge – Ohio   *Rothstein for F.S.A.*

Wisconsin Silo   *Vories Fisher*

FAIR IS OUR LAND

Pumpkin Pattern

Ewing Galloway

Harvest in Pennsylvania *Delano for F.S.A.*

March Winds *J. H. Thomas*

Feeding Time – Iowa   *Rothstein for F.S.A.*

Kansas Corn   *Keystone*

Cloudy Sky   *Etching by John E. Costigan*

Early Planting   *Etching by Kerr Eby*

Sunset – Imperial, Nebraska   *Rothstein for F.S.A.*

Nebraska Loam   *Rothstein for F.S.A.*
THE FARM

Colorado Foothills   *Lee for F.S.A.*

The Thresher – Utah   *Lee for F.S.A.*

FAIR IS OUR LAND

Split Rail Fence – Muncie, Indiana *Ewing Galloway*

Farm Pattern in Iowa *Rothstein for F.S.A.*

Sheep Ranch in Oregon   *Rothstein for F.S.A.*

Oregon Pastorale   *Ray Atkeson*

Sixteen Horse Combine – Eastern Washington   *Rothstein for F.S.A.*

The Palouse Wheat Country – Washington   *Rothstein for F.S.A.*

THE FARM

Lettuce Factory – Salinas, California   *Orville Logan*

North Powder Valley Farm – Oregon   *Minor White*

FAIR IS OUR LAND

Paysage   *Pierson Studio*

The Countryside

IN THE EAST AND SOUTH

Village in the Hills – East Corinth, Vermont *Ewing Galloway*

Salt Marshes *Etching by Kerr Eby*

FAIR IS OUR LAND

The Gladstone Road – Winter   *Thomas O. Sheckell*

Saunderstown Fields   *Drypoint by Samuel Chamberlain*

THE COUNTRYSIDE

Winter Shadows – Stowe, Vermont   *Marion Post Wolcott for F.S.A.*

Haying Time in Vermont   *Tet Borsig*

New England Winter – Essex, Massachusetts *Samuel Chamberlain*

Sunlit Forest *Lithograph by Stow Wengenroth*

THE COUNTRYSIDE

Maples in Early Spring   *Etching by Childe Hassam*

FAIR IS OUR LAND

Cider Mill   *Etching by Kerr Eby*

The Old Farm   *Etching by C. W. Anderson*

Covered Bridge   *Frank R. Fraprie*

New England Road   *Etching by C. W. Anderson*

Crossroads – North Andover, Massachusetts   *Samuel Chamberlain*

Snow and Mist   *Etching by Robert Nisbet*

THE COUNTRYSIDE

The Start of the Day   *Etching by A. L. Ripley*

Landscape   *Etching by C. W. Anderson*

Spring Road – Rochester, New Hampshire   *Samuel Chamberlain*

Snowscape – Beverly, Massachusetts   *Samuel Chamberlain*

Sugaring-off Time – North Bridgewater, Vermont   *Marion Post Wolcott for F.S.A.*

Vermont Valley – near Rutland   *Marion Post Wolcott for F.S.A.*

Skier's Heaven – New Hampshire   *H. E. Adams for U. S. Forest Service*

Winter Hillside – Woodstock, Vermont   *Marion Post Wolcott for F.S.A.*

THE COUNTRYSIDE

Haying Time – Windsor, Vermont   *Rothstein for F.S.A.*

Winter Landscape – Woodstock, Vermont   *Marion Post Wolcott for F.S.A.*

Road on the Housitanic – New Milford, Connecticut   *Ewing Galloway*

Midsummer – Woodbury, Connecticut   *Samuel Chamberlain*

THE COUNTRYSIDE

Nocturne

Pierson Studio

FAIR IS OUR LAND

Morning After A Snowstorm – Essex, Massachusetts *Samuel Chamberlain*

Shady Valley *Etching by R. W. Waiceske*

Windmill – Easthampton, Long Island

Tet Borsig

FAIR IS OUR LAND

The Old Swimming Hole – Pine Grove Mills, Pennsylvania *Rosskam for F.S.A.*

Ohio Landscape *Rothstein for F.S.A.*

THE COUNTRYSIDE

Silver Frost in the Adirondacks   *Gustav Anderson*

Thanksgiving Time   *Etching by Peter Marcus*

Minnesota Forest   *Leland J. Prater for U. S. Forest Service*

THE COUNTRYSIDE

Footloose – Locust Valley, Long Island *Tet Borsig*

Cherry Blossoms in Washington *Browning*

FAIR IS OUR LAND

Early Spring – Tiverton, Rhode Island   *Samuel Chamberlain*

White Face Mountain   *Pierson Studio*

THE COUNTRYSIDE

Fruit Blossoms – Aberdeen, Maryland *Samuel Chamberlain*

Moonshiner's Cabin *Etching by Chauncey F. Ryder*

FAIR IS OUR LAND

Cloud Spots on the Skyline Drive – Virginia   *Samuel Chamberlain*

Silhouette   *Arthur Hammond*

THE COUNTRYSIDE

Greenwood Portico – A Louisiana Plantation   *Frances Benjamin Johnston*

Avenue of Live Oaks – Oak Alley, Louisiana   *Frances Benjamin Johnston*

Early Sugar Mill – Orange City, Florida   *Frances Benjamin Johnston*

THE COUNTRYSIDE

The Country Road – South Carolina   *Marion Post Wolcott for F.S.A.*

Church in the Cornfields – Manning, South Carolina *Marion P. Wolcott for F.S.A.*

Southern Giant   *Tet Borsig*

The Swamps   *Tet Borsig*

Rappahannock Hills – Virginia   *Rothstein for F.S.A.*

Evergreen Horizon – Virginia   *Rothstein for F.S.A.*

Kentucky Farm Estate *Marion Post Wolcott for F.S.A.*

Spring Morning – Shenandoah Valley, Virginia *Marion P. Wolcott for F.S.A.*

Spring on a Long Island Farm   *Gustav Anderson*

Entrance to Monument Valley   *Cedric Wright*

The Great West

Country Church in Iowa   *Vachon for F.S.A.*

Highway No. 16 – South Dakota   *Ewing Galloway*

Farm Road in North Dakota   *Vachon for F.S.A.*

Country School – Ward County, North Dakota   *Vachon for F.S.A.*

The Foothills in Colorado   *Lee for F.S.A*

The Plains of South Dakota   *Vachon for F.S.A*

Montana Sheepherder   *Rothstein for F.S.A.*

Colorado Pasture   *Rothstein for F.S.A.*

Cattle Range – Montana   *F. E. Dunham for U. S. Forest Service*

Round-up – Montana   *Rothstein for F.S.A.*

Sheepherder's Camp   *Paul S. Bieler for U. S. Forest Service*

Sheep Country – Eastern Washington   *Ray Atkeson*

Four Moods of Monument Valley – I. Sunrise   *Josef Muench*

II. Mid-day   *Ernest Knee*

III. Afternoon   *Josef Muench*

IV. Sunset   *Cedric Wright*

THE GREAT WEST

Three Circle Round-up – Montana   *Rothstein for F.S.A.*

Valley Ranch in Utah   *Ray Atkeson*

FAIR IS OUR LAND

The Corral – Jackson, Wyoming   *Rothstein for F.S.A.*

Desert Bloom   *Chuck Abbott*

Road to the Desert – Utah
Rothstein for F.S.A.

Hopi Village
Chuck Abbott

Tailings Pit of the Gold Mill – Telluride, Colorado *Lee for F.S.A.*

Grand Junction Valley – Colorado *Josef Muench*

Desert Flowers

Esther Henderson

FAIR IS OUR LAND

Hay Stacker – Utah   *Rothstein for F.S.A.*

South Park Colorado in Winter   *Charles B. Abbott*

The Round-up – New Mexico   *W. H. Shaffer for U.S. Forest Servic*

Northern New Mexico   *Ernest Kne*

Approaching Storm – Santa Fe, New Mexico   *Ernest Knee*

San Xavier Mission – New Mexico   *Esther Henderson*

Betatakin Cliff Dwellings – Navajo National Monument   *Hubert A. Lowman*

Natural Bridge – Arches National Monument   *Hubert A. Lowman*

Cliff Dwellers Village – Canyon de Chelly   *Hubert A. Lowman*

THE GREAT WEST   135

The Desert by Day   *Hubert A. Lowman*

Night in the Apache Desert   *Aquatint by Arthur Hall*

Sand Dunes – Yuma, Arizona *Hubert A. Lowman*

Indian Houses – Salt River *Etching by George Elbert Burr*

"Elephant's Feet" – Near Red Lake, Arizona   *Josef Muench*

Navajo Sheep in Monument Valley   *Chuck Abbott*

Light Snows in Utah

Lee for F.S.A.

Fertile Valley – San Cristobal, New Mexico

Lee for F.S.A.

THE GREAT WEST

Cactus Country

140   FAIR IS OUR LAND

Yucca and Wildflowers   *Chuck Abbott*

Desert Nocturne   *Josef Muench*

Bright Angel Point – Grand Canyon

Hubert A. Lowman

FAIR IS OUR LAND

The Grand Canyon   *Department of the Interior*

Dead Wood – Grand Canyon   *Cedric Wright*

THE GREAT WEST   143

The Bright Angel Trail – Grand Canyon   *Lithograph by Joseph Pennell*

South Rim of the Grand Canyon   *Laura Gilpin*

Early Morning in the Grand Canyon   *Ernest Knee*

Mitchell Pass – Scotts Bluff National Monument   *Geo. A. Grant for Dept. of the Int.*

Bryce Canyon   *Laura Gilpin*

Desert Sycamore   *Esther Henderson*

Santa Anita Pass *Etching by R. Stephens Wright*

Logging Camp in Oregon *Lee for F.S.A.*

Elk Hunters   *Etching by Levon West*

Coastal Pastures – California   *Grant Duggins*

Death Valley Dunes

Geo. A. Grant for U.S. Dept. of the Interior

Death Valley – California

Grant Duggins

Storm on East Escapement – Sierra Nevada   *Cedric Wright*

Grande Ronde Valley – Oregon *Minor White*

Sky Pastures *Roi Partridge*

The Library – University of Virginia   *Samuel Chamberlain*

Our Architectural Inheritance

Springtime in Salem   *Drypoint by Samuel Chamberlain*

Weathered Clapboards   *Samuel Chamberlain*

Church on the Green – Middlebury, Vermont   *Samuel Chamberlain*

OUR ARCHITECTURAL INHERITANCE   155

The Parson Capen House – Topsfield, Massachusetts   *Samuel Chamberlain*

FAIR IS OUR LAND

Longfellow's Wayside Inn – South Sudbury, Massachusetts *Samuel Chamberlain*

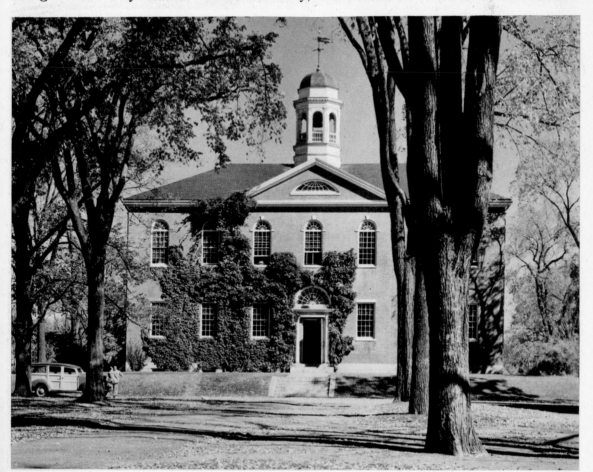

Bulfinch Hall – Andover, Massachusetts *Samuel Chamberlain*

Old Buildings in Harvard Yard – Cambridge, Massachusetts   *Samuel Chamberlain*

The State House – Boston, Massachusetts   *Samuel Chamberlain*

Independence Hall – Philadelphia, Pennsylvania   *Ewing Galloway*

The Capitol Dome – Washington, D.C.   *Ewing Galloway*

Mount Vernon *Frances Benjamin Johnston*

The White House *Delano for F.S.A.*

OUR ARCHITECTURAL INHERITANCE

The Apothecary's Shop – Williamsburg, Virginia *Drypoint by Samuel Chamberlain*

FAIR IS OUR LAND

Monticello – Near Charlottesville, Virginia   *Samuel Chamberlain*

The Capitol – Williamsburg, Virginia   *Drypoint by Samuel Chamberlain*

Springtime in Williamsburg   *Richard Garrison*

Otwell – Maryland   *Frances Benjamin Johnston*

Sweet Hall – Virginia   *Frances Benjamin Johnston*

OUR ARCHITECTURAL INHERITANCE

Blacklock House – Charleston, South Carolina

Frances Benjamin Johnston

FAIR IS OUR LAND

Church Street – Charleston, South Carolina   *Frances Benjamin Johnston*

Ruins of Sheldon Church – South Carolina   *Frances Benjamin Johnston*

General Bragg's House – Mobile, Alabama   *Frances Benjamin Johnston*

Past Glory – Bellegrove, Louisiana   *Frances Benjamin Johnston*

Upson House – Athens, Georgia   *Frances Benjamin Johnston*

Belle Helena Plantation – Louisiana   *Vories Fisher*

Greenwood Plantation – Louisiana   *Frances Benjamin Johnston*

FAIR IS OUR LAND

The Hermitage – Plantation in Louisiana   *Vories Fisher*

Courtyard in the Vieux Carré – New Orleans   *Frances Benjamin Johnston*

The Old State Capitol – Des Moines, Iowa *Ewing Galloway*

The Conception Mission – near San Antonio, Texas *Underwood-Stratton*

FAIR IS OUR LAND

Mission San Jose – San Antonio   *Claude B. Aniol*

The Alamo – San Antonio   *Claude B. Aniol*

OUR ARCHITECTURAL INHERITANCE

Tumacacori Mission – Arizona   *Hubert A. Lowman*

Old Spanish Mission – Taos, New Mexico   *Rothstein for F.S.A.*

Mission San Xavier – Arizona

Josef Muench

Mission San Xavier – Arizona

Esther Henderson

OUR ARCHITECTURAL INHERITANCE

Far West Architecture – Virginia City, Nevada   *Rothstein for F.S.A.*

Old Courthouse – Tombstone, Arizona   *Chuck Abbott*

San Juan Bautista Mission

Will Connell

Santa Barbara Mission

Will Connell

Santa Ynez Mission *Grant Duggins*

San Luis Rey Mission *Grant Duggins*

Yosemite Falls   *Padilla Studios*

Mountain Ranges
and the Nation's Parks

Estes Park – Colorado

Tet Borsig

Pike's Peak Beyond A Screen of Saplings

Laura Gilpin

FAIR IS OUR LAND

Mt. Cannon – Montana   *Hileman for Glacier National Park*

MOUNTAIN RANGES AND THE NATION'S PARKS

The Mountains in White   *Fritz Kaeser*

The Mountains in Black – West Gate   *Etching by Levon West*

Wintry Silhouette · *Josef Muench*

MOUNTAIN RANGES AND THE NATION'S PARKS · · · · · · · · · · · · · · · · · 183

Goat Mountain – Montana   *Hileman for Glacier National Park*

The Peak   *Etching by Levon West*

The Mission Range – Montana   *U.S. Forest Service*

The Bad Lands – South Dakota   *Ewing Galloway*

MOUNTAIN RANGES AND THE NATION'S PARKS

Wallowa Mountains – Oregon   *Minor White*

Carson Pass – California   *McCurry*

San Francisco Peaks – Arizona *Esther Henderson*

MOUNTAIN RANGES AND THE NATION'S PARKS

The Sierras in Midwinter   *Josef Muench*

Mount Shasta   *Ray Atkeson*

Mount Hood   *Ray Atkeson*

Shuksan in Winter   *Etching by Helen A. Loggie*

Mount Hood   *Ray Atkeson*

The Cascade Range – Washington   *Ray Atkeson*

FAIR IS OUR LAND

Trail Approaching Mount Whitney   *Cedric Wright*

Sunset from Muir Pass – California   *Cedric Wright*

MOUNTAIN RANGES AND THE NATION'S PARKS

Peak of Mount Hood in the Clouds *Ray Atkeson*

Midwinter on Mount Hood *Ray Atkeson*

FAIR IS OUR LAND

Drift Snow   *Josef Muench*

Reflections in the High Sierra   *Josef Muench*

MOUNTAIN RANGES AND THE NATION'S PARKS   193

Autumn Snow on Mount Adams   *Ray Atkeson*

Alpine Meadows – Mount Rainier   *U.S. Department of the Interior*

FAIR IS OUR LAND

Deadwood Drama – Mount Rainier

U.S. Department of the Interior

The Gates of Yosemite Valley   *Ansel Adams for U.S. Department of the Interior*

Yosemite Valley After a Snow Storm   *Ralph Anderson for U.S. Dept. of the Int.*

FAIR IS OUR LAND

Sequoias in the Snow   *Ralph Anderson for U.S. Department of the Interior*

MOUNTAIN RANGES AND THE NATION'S PARKS

El Capitan – Yosemite Valley

U.S. Department of the Interior

FAIR IS OUR LAND

Horse Ridge – Yosemite National Park   *U.S. Department of the Interior*

Half Dome – Yosemite National Park   *Padilla Studios for U.S. Dept. of the Interior*

Gunsight Lake   *Hileman for Glacier National Park*

Temple of Tinawana – Zion National Park   *Geo. A. Grant for U.S. Dept. of Interior*

Grinnell Glacier *Hileman for Glacier National Park*

Glacier Lillies – Mount Clements *Hileman for Glacier National Park*

Bear Grass – Mount Gould   *Hileman for U.S. Department of the Interior*

Badger Pass in Winter – Yosemite   *Ansel Adams for U.S. Department of the Interior*

FAIR IS OUR LAND

Mountain Highway   *Hileman for Glacier National Park*

Blue Pools on Jupiter Terrace – Yellowstone National Park   *Ray Atkeson*

MOUNTAIN RANGES AND THE NATION'S PARKS   203

The Monarchs – Sequoia National Park *U.S. Department of the Interior*

FAIR IS OUR LAND

Forest Giants   *Gabriel Moulin for U.S. Department of the Interior*

Sunburst   *Ray Atkeson*

Cape Elizabeth – Maine   *Ewing Galloway*

The Seacoasts

Smoke Houses – Thomaston, Maine   *Samuel Chamberlain*

Portland Head Light – Maine   *Ewing Galloway*

FAIR IS OUR LAND

Lobsterman's Cove   *Lithograph by Stow Wengenroth*

After the Rain   *Lithograph by Stow Wengenroth*

Seine Boats – Gloucester, Massachusetts   *Samuel Chamberlain*

Rocky Neck – Gloucester   *Etching by Max Kuehn*

The Old Whaler "Charles W. Morgan" *Samuel Chamberlain*

Boats At Dawn *Etching by Frank W. Benson*

THE SEACOASTS

The Cliffs of Gay Head – Matha's Vineyard, Massachusetts   *Samuel Chamberlain*

The Gunner's Blind   *Etching by Frank W. Benson*

Race Week – Marblehead, Massachusetts   *Samuel Chamberlain*

Portsmouth Harbor – New Hampshire   *Etching by Charles H. Woodbury*

THE SEACOASTS

Stonington Sunset – Connecticut

Drypoint by Samuel Chamberlain

Coast Storm

Etching by C. Jac Young

FAIR IS OUR LAND

Coming In   *Etching by C. Jac Young*

"Motif No. 1" – Rockport, Massachusetts   *Gerhard H. Bakker*

THE SEACOASTS

Black Squall

Eleanor Park Custis

FAIR IS OUR LAND

Seine Fishermen   *Eleanor Park Custis*

The Dunes – Montauk Point, Long Island   *Tet Borsig*

Net Pattern – Long Island   *Tet Borsig*

Reflections in Boston Harbor

Frank R. Fraprie

The Shore At Montauk Point – Long Island

Tet Borsig

FAIR IS OUR LAND

Oyster Boats – Cape Cod   *Ralph E. Day*

Lower Manhattan – Seen by the Camera   *Ewing Galloway*

Lower Manhattan – Seen by the Lithographer   *Lithograph by Joseph Pennell*

FAIR IS OUR LAND

The Queen and Her Slaves   *Etching by Otto Kuhler*

Civic Insomnia   *Aquatint by Gerald K. Geerlings*

THE SEACOASTS

The Spires of Manhattan   *Etching by Otto Kuhler*

New York Harbor   *Tet Borsig*

Delaware Fishing Village *Vachon for F.S.A.*

Oyster Boats in Deal's Island Bay *Delano for F.S.A.*

Shores of Maryland   *Soft Ground Etching by F. Townsend Morgan*

Fishing Fleet – Hampton, Virginia   *Samuel Chamberlain*

FAIR IS OUR LAND

Windswept   *Etching by Alfred Hutty*

Sand Dunes – St. Augustine, Florida *Arthur Hammond*

Beach Grass – Florida *Arthur Hammond*

FAIR IS OUR LAND

The Breakers   *Ray Atkeson*

THE SEACOASTS

Wings Against The Sky – Mississippi *Anthony V. Ragusir*

The Oyster Fleet – Biloxi, Mississippi *Anthony V. Ragusir*

Florida Shore   *Arthur Hammond*

Pacific Sands *Brett Weston*

California Surf *Robert Ingram*

Fish Harbor *Etching by R. Stephens Wright*

Snug Harbor *Etching by Armin Hanson*

THE SEACOASTS

Small Mission Wharf   *Etching by John W. Winkler*

View from Telegraph Hill – San Francisco   *Etching by John W. Winkler*

Fishermen's Wharf – San Francisco   *Robert Ingram*

Puget Sound – Washington *Etching by R. Stephens Wright*

Venice in Oakland *Roi Patridge*

FAIR IS OUR LAND

Compositon at Low Tide   *Roi Partridge*

Arch Cape – Oregon

Ray Atkeson

FAIR IS OUR LAND

Cape Kiwanda – Oregon *Ray Atkeson*

Cannon Beach – Oregon *Ray Atkeson*

THE SEACOASTS

The Pacific   *Roi Patridge*

STONE BARN   *Wood Engraving by Thomas W. Nason*

List of Illustrations

TITLE	MEDIUM	ARTIST	PAGE
A BUCKS COUNTY FARMHOUSE	Wood Engraving	Thomas W. Nason	9
WINDSWEPT	Woodcut	Thomas W. Nason	17
BERKSHIRE HILLS	Wood Engraving	Thomas W. Nason	21
BLACKSMITH'S SHOP	Woodcut	Thomas W. Nason	22
TOWNS AND VILLAGES			
POWNAL, VERMONT	Photograph	Gustav Anderson	25
MIDWINTER, WEST HARTFORD, VERMONT	Photograph	Marion Post Wolcott for Farm Security Administration	26
WOODEN GOTHIC, LANCASTER, N.H.	Photograph	Rothstein for F.S.A.	26
THE FRARY HOUSE—OLD DEERFIELD, MASS.	Photograph	Samuel Chamberlain	27
BERKSHIRE NIGHT	Etching	Kerr Eby	27

SUMMER STREET	Drypoint	Samuel Chamberlain	28
BEND IN THE ROAD, NEWCASTLE, N.H.	Drypoint	Samuel Chamberlain	29
SPRINGTIME IN THE VILLAGE, PETERBURG, NEW YORK	Photograph	Keystone	29
NORTHERNMOST NEW ENGLAND, FORT KENT, MAINE	Photograph	Delano for F.S.A.	30
NEW ENGLAND NIGHT	Lithograph	C. W. Anderson	30
CORNWALL BRIDGE	Etching	Armin Landeck	31
EASTHAMPTON, LONG ISLAND	Photograph	Tet Borsig	31
PORCH LIGHT—PIERRE, SOUTH DAKOTA	Photograph	Vachon for F.S.A.	32
MAIN STREET—GRUNDY CENTER, IOWA	Photograph	Rothstein for F.S.A.	32
MRS. ELLIS' STORE—FALMOUTH, VA.	Photograph	Frances Benjamin Johnston	33
PRAIRIE VILLAGE—SURREY, NORTH DAKOTA	Photograph	Vachon for F.S.A.	34
TANK TOWN—BRIDGEPORT, WISCONSIN	Photograph	Vachon for F.S.A.	34
COLORADO HILL TOWN—OURAY	Photograph	Rothstein for F.S.A.	35
GHOST TOWN—EUREKA, COLORADO	Photograph	Lee for F.S.A.	36
SILVERTON—COLORADO	Photograph	Lee for F.S.A.	36
SILVER PEAK, NEVADA	Photograph	Rothstein for F.S.A.	37
PRE-HISTORIC VILLAGE—MESA VERDE	Photograph	Cedric Wright	37
MONTANA PRAIRIE TOWN	Photograph	Rothstein for F.S.A.	38
PUEBLO VILLAGE—TAOS, NEW MEXICO	Photograph	Rothstein for F.S.A.	38

INLAND WATERS

HINCKLEY LAKE—OHIO	Photograph	Ewing Galloway	39
LAKE IN THE HILLS—NORTH CAROLINA	Photograph	Ewing Galloway	40
SUNSET ON NEWFOUND LAKE, N.H.	Photograph	Arthur Hammond	41
SAND DUNES ON LAKE MICHIGAN	Photograph	Underwood & Underwood	41
TRAPPER'S LAKE—COLORADO	Photograph	U.S. Forest Service	42
LAKE TARRYALL	Lithograph	Adolph Dehn	42
TILDEN LAKE—YOSEMITE NATIONAL PARK	Photograph	Cedric Wright	43
KLAMATH LAKE—OREGON	Photograph	Ray Atkeson	44
SPIRIT LAKE AND MT. ST. HELENS	Photograph	Ray Atkeson	44
GOLD MILL—COLORADO	Photograph	Lee for F.S.A.	45
SAN CARLOS LAKE—ARIZONA	Photograph	Josef Muench	45
ST. MARY'S LAKE—GLACIER NATIONAL PARK	Photograph	U.S. Dept. of the Interior	46
SEVEN LAKES BASIN—OLYMPIC NATIONAL PARK	Photograph	Asahel Curtis for U.S. Dept. of the Interior	46
CRATER LAKE—OREGON	Photograph	Ray Atkeson	47
LOST LAKE—OREGON	Photograph	Ray Atkeson	47
TRICK FALLS—GLACIER NATIONAL PARK	Photograph	Hileman	48

Niagara Falls	Photograph	Ewing Galloway	49
The Dam at Pigeon Forge—Tennessee	Photograph	Ewing Galloway	49
Punch Bowl Falls—Oregon	Photograph	C. M. Ballard for U.S. Forest Service	50
Swift Current Falls—Montana	Photograph	Hileman for Glacier National Park	50
Glen Aulin Falls—California	Photograph	Cedric Wright	51
River Bend in Provo Canyon—Utah	Photograph	Ray Atkeson	51
The York River—Maine	Etching	R. Stephens Wright	52
Curiosity	Etching	Frank Besedick	52
The Sweeping Ohio	Photograph	B. W. Muir for U.S. Forest Service	53
Steamboat on the Kentucky River	Photograph	Ewing Galloway	53
West Point	Etching	Gerald K. Geerlings	54
Mississippi Evening	Etching	Otto Kuhler	54
The Amy Hewes—Louisiana	Photograph	Ewing Galloway	55
Mississippi River Ferry, Helena, Ark.	Photograph	Arkansas State Publicity Dept.	55
The Colorado River	Photograph	Hubert A. Lowman	56
North Platte River—Nebraska	Photograph	Underwood & Underwood	56
High Water on the Sacramento River	Photograph	Grant Duggins	57
The Columbia River Gorge	Photograph	Ray Atkeson	58
Indian Salmon Fishermen—Columbia River	Photograph	Ray Atkeson	58

THE FARM

The Grande Ronde Valley—Oregon	Photograph	Minor White	59
A Pennsylvania Landscape	Wood Engraving	Thomas Nason	60
Farm on the River	Drypoint	Chauncey F. Ryder	60
August Afternoon on the Farm, Rowley, Massachusetts	Photograph	Samuel Chamberlain	61
Hilltop	Photograph	Eleanor Park Custis	61
Barns in Winter—Putney, Vermont	Photograph	Marion Post Wolcott for F.S.A.	62
The Casey Farm—North Kingston, R.I.	Photograph	Samuel Chamberlain	62
Abandoned Farm, Hampton Falls, N.H.	Photograph	Samuel Chamberlain	63
Hay Cutting Time in Vermont	Photograph	Rothstein for F.S.A.	63
New England Farm on the Merrimac	Photograph	Eleanor Park Custis	64
Pennsylvania Farmland	Photograph	Marion Post Wolcott for F.S.A.	65
Harvest in Ohio	Photograph	Ewing Galloway	65
Farm on the Atlantic Shore, Gloucester, Mass.	Photograph	Samuel Chamberlain	66

LIST OF ILLUSTRATIONS

Barns of Purissima	Photograph	C. Stanton Loeber	66
String Bean Pickers—Cambridge, Md.	Photograph	Rothstein for F.S.A.	67
Barn with Stone Silos	Photograph	Henry Flannery	67
Log Farm House—Roanoke, Virginia	Photograph	Frances Benjamin Johnston	68
Old Slave Quarters—Kendall Grove, Eastville, Virginia	Photograph	Frances Benjamin Johnston	68
Upland Farms of Virginia—Autumn, Near Marion, Virginia	Photograph	Marion Post Wolcott for F.S.A.	69
Upland Farms of Virginia—Winter, Rappahannock County	Photograph	Rothstein for F.S.A.	69
Tobacco Field in the Kentucky Mountains	Photograph	Marion Post Wolcott for F.S.A.	70
Tobacco Harvest	Photograph	Marion Post Wolcott for F.S.A.	70
Contrasting Farms in Kentucky—the Backwoods	Photograph	Marion Post Wolcott for F.S.A.	71
Dairy Farm in Jefferson County, Ky.	Photograph	Marion Post Wolcott for F.S.A.	71
Mississippi Mule Team	Photograph	Marion Post Wolcott for F.S.A.	72
Cotton Picking Time—Benoit, Miss.	Photograph	Marion Post Wolcott for F.S.A.	72
The Fertile Earth	Lithograph	Albert W. Barker	73
Foot Bridge—Ohio	Photograph	Rothstein for F.S.A.	74
Wisconsin Silo	Photograph	Vories Fisher	74
Pumpkin Pattern	Photograph	Ewing Galloway	75
Harvest in Pennsylvania	Photograph	Delano for F.S.A.	76
March Winds	Photograph	J. H. Thomas	76
Feeding Time—Iowa	Photograph	Rothstein for F.S.A.	77
Kansas Corn	Photograph	Keystone	77
Cloudy Sky	Etching	John E. Costigan	78
Early Planting	Etching	Kerr Eby	78
Sunset—Imperial, Nebraska	Photograph	Rothstein for F.S.A.	79
Nebraska Loam	Photograph	Rothstein for F.S.A.	79
Colorado Foothills	Photograph	Lee for F.S.A.	80
The Thresher—Utah	Photograph	Lee for F.S.A.	80
Split Rail Fence—Muncie, Indiana	Photograph	Ewing Galloway	81
Farm Pattern in Iowa	Photograph	Rothstein for F.S.A.	81
Sheep Ranch in Oregon	Photograph	Rothstein for F.S.A.	82
Oregon Pastorale	Photograph	Ray Atkeson	82
Sixteen Horse Combine—Eastern Washington	Photograph	Rothstein for F.S.A.	83
The Palouse Wheat Country—Washington	Photograph	Rothstein for F.S.A.	83

LETTUCE FACTORY—SALINAS, CAL.	Photograph	Orville Logan Snider	84
NORTH POWDER VALLEY FARM—OREGON	Photograph	Minor White	84

THE COUNTRYSIDE IN THE EAST AND SOUTH

PAYSAGE	Photograph	Pierson Studio	85
VILLAGE IN THE HILLS—EAST CORINTH, VERMONT	Photograph	Ewing Galloway	86
SALT MARSHES	Etching	Kerr Eby	86
THE GLADSTONE ROAD—WINTER	Photograph	Thomas O. Sheckell	87
SAUNDERSTOWN FIELDS	Drypoint	Samuel Chamberlain	87
WINTER SHADOWS—STOWE, VERMONT	Photograph	Marion Post Wolcott for F.S.A.	88
HAYING TIME IN VERMONT	Photograph	Tet Borsig	88
NEW ENGLAND WINTER—ESSEX, MASS.	Photograph	Samuel Chamberlain	89
SUNLIT FOREST	Lithograph	Stow Wengenroth	89
MAPLES IN EARLY SPRING	Etching	Childe Hassam	90
CIDER MILL	Etching	Kerr Eby	91
THE OLD FARM	Etching	C. W. Anderson	91
COVERED BRIDGE	Photograph	Frank R. Fraprie	92
NEW ENGLAND ROAD	Etching	C. W. Anderson	92
CROSSROADS—NORTH ANDOVER, MASS.	Photograph	Samuel Chamberlain	93
SNOW AND MIST	Etching	Robert Nesbit	93
THE START OF THE DAY	Etching	A. L. Ripley	94
LANDSCAPE	Etching	C. W. Anderson	94
SPRING ROAD—ROCHESTER, N.H.	Photograph	Samuel Chamberlain	95
SNOWSCAPE—BEVERLY, MASS.	Photograph	Samuel Chamberlain	95
SUGARING-OFF TIME—NORTH BRIDGE-WATER, VERMONT	Photograph	Marion Post Wolcott for F.S.A.	96
VERMONT VALLEY—NEAR RUTLAND	Photograph	Marion Post Wolcott for F.S.A.	96
SKIERS' HEAVEN—NEW HAMPSHIRE	Photograph	H. E. Adams for U.S. Forest Service	97
WINTER HILLSIDE—WOODSTOCK, VT.	Photograph	Marion Post Wolcott for F.S.A.	97
HAYING TIME—WINDSOR, VERMONT	Photograph	Rothstein for F.S.A.	98
WINTER LANDSCAPE—WOODSTOCK, VT.	Photograph	Marion Post Wolcott for F.S.A.	98
ROAD ON THE HOUSATONIC, NEW MILFORD, CONNECTICUT	Photograph	Ewing Galloway	99
MIDSUMMER—WOODBURY, CONNECTICUT	Photograph	Samuel Chamberlain	99
NOCTURNE	Photograph	Pierson Studio	100
MORNING AFTER A SNOWSTORM—ESSEX, MASS.	Photograph	Samuel Chamberlain	101

SHADY VALLEY	Etching	R. W. Woiceske	101
WINDMILL—EASTHAMPTON, L.I.	Photograph	Tet Borsig	102
THE OLD SWIMMING HOLE—PINE GROVE MILLS, PENNSYLVANIA	Photograph	Rosskam for F.S.A.	103
OHIO LANDSCAPE	Photograph	Rothstein for F.S.A.	103
SILVER FROST IN THE ADIRONDACKS	Photograph	Gustav Anderson	104
THANKSGIVING TIME	Etching	Peter Marcus	105
MINNESOTA FOREST	Photograph	Leland J. Prater for U.S. Forest Service	105
FOOTLOOSE—LOCUST VALLEY, L.I.	Photograph	Tet Borsig	106
CHERRY BLOSSOMS IN WASHINGTON	Photograph	Browning	106
EARLY SPRING—TIVERTON, R.I.	Photograph	Samuel Chamberlain	107
WHITE FACE MOUNTAIN	Photograph	Pierson Studio	107
FRUIT BLOSSOMS—ABERDEEN, MD.	Photograph	Samuel Chamberlain	108
MOONSHINER'S CABIN	Etching	Chauncey F. Ryder	108
CLOUD SPOTS ALONG THE SKYLINE DRIVE, VIRGINIA	Photograph	Samuel Chamberlain	109
SILHOUETTE	Photograph	Arthur Hammond	109
GREENWOOD PORTICO—A LOUISIANA PLANTATION	Photograph	Frances Benjamin Johnston	110
AVENUE OF LIVE OAKS—OAK ALLEY, LOUISIANA	Photograph	Frances Benjamin Johnston	111
EARLY SUGAR MILL—ORANGE CITY, FLA.	Photograph	Frances Benjamin Johnston	111
THE COUNTRY ROAD—SOUTH CAROLINA	Photograph	Marion Post Wolcott for F.S.A.	112
CHURCH IN THE CORNFIELDS, MANNING, SOUTH CAROLINA	Photograph	Marion Post Wolcott for F.S.A.	112
SOUTHERN GIANT	Photograph	Tet Borsig	113
THE SWAMPS	Photograph	Tet Borsig	113
RAPPAHANNOCK HILLS—VIRGINIA	Photograph	Rothstein for F.S.A.	114
EVERGREEN HORIZON—VIRGINIA	Photograph	Rothstein for F.S.A.	114
KENTUCKY FARM ESTATE	Photograph	Marion Post Wolcott for F.S.A.	115
SPRING MORNING IN THE SHENANDOAH VALLEY—VIRGINIA	Photograph	Marion Post Wolcott for F.S.A.	115
SPRING ON A LONG ISLAND FARM	Photograph	Gustav Anderson	116

THE GREAT WEST

ENTRANCE TO MONUMENT VALLEY	Photograph	Cedric Wright	117
COUNTRY CHURCH IN IOWA	Photograph	Vachon for F.S.A.	118
HIGHWAY No. 16—SOUTH DAKOTA	Photograph	Ewing Galloway	118
FARM ROAD IN NORTH DAKOTA	Photograph	Vachon for F.S.A.	119
COUNTRY SCHOOL—WARD COUNTY, N.D.	Photograph	Vachon for F.S.A.	119

THE FOOTHILLS IN COLORADO	Photograph	Lee for F.S.A.	120
THE PLAINS OF SOUTH DAKOTA	Photograph	Vachon for F.S.A.	120
MONTANA SHEEPHERDER	Photograph	Rothstein for F.S.A.	121
COLORADO PASTURE	Photograph	Rothstein for F.S.A.	121
CATTLE RANGE—MONTANA	Photograph	F. E. Dunham for U.S. Forest Service	122
ROUNDUP—MONTANA	Photograph	Rothstein for F.S.A.	122
SHEEPHERDER'S CAMP	Photograph	Paul S. Bieler for U.S. Forest Service	123
SHEEP COUNTRY—EASTERN WASHINGTON	Photograph	Ray Atkeson	123
FOUR MOODS OF MONUMENT VALLEY			
I.—SUNRISE	Photograph	Josef Muench	124
II.—MID-DAY	Photograph	Ernest Knee	124
III.—AFTERNOON	Photograph	Josef Muench	125
IV.—SUNSET	Photograph	Cedric Wright	125
THREE CIRCLE ROUNDUP—MONTANA	Photograph	Rothstein for F.S.A.	126
VALLEY RANCH IN UTAH	Photograph	Ray Atkeson	126
THE CORAL—JACKSON, WYOMING	Photograph	Rothstein for F.S.A.	127
DESERT BLOOM	Photograph	Chuck Abbott	127
ROAD TO THE DESERT—UTAH	Photograph	Rothstein for F.S.A.	128
HOPI VILLAGE	Photograph	Chuck Abbott	128
TAILINGS PIT OF THE GOLD MILL, TELLURIDE, COLORADO	Photograph	Lee for F.S.A.	129
GRAND JUNCTION VALLEY—COLORADO	Photograph	Josef Muench	129
DESERT FLOWERS	Photograph	Esther Henderson	130
HAY STACKER—UTAH	Photograph	Rothstein for F.S.A.	131
SOUTH PARK COLORADO IN WINTER	Photograph	Charles B. Abbott	131
THE ROUNDUP—NEW MEXICO	Photograph	W. H. Shaffer for U.S. Forest Service	132
NORTHERN NEW MEXICO	Photograph	Ernest Knee	132
APPROACHING STORM—SANTA FE, N.M.	Photograph	Ernest Knee	133
SAN XAVIER MISSION—NEW MEXICO	Photograph	Esther Henderson	133
BETATAKIN CLIFF DWELLINGS—NAVAJO NATIONAL MONUMENT	Photograph	Hubert A. Lowman	134
NATURAL BRIDGE—ARCHES NATIONAL MONUMENT	Photograph	Hubert A. Lowman	134
CLIFF DWELLERS VILLAGE—CANYON DE CHELLY	Photograph	Hubert A. Lowman	135
THE DESERT BY DAY	Photograph	Hubert A. Lowman	136
NIGHT IN THE APACHE DESERT	Aquatint	Arthur Hall	136
SAND DUNES—YUMA, ARIZONA	Photograph	Hubert A. Lowman	137
INDIAN HOUSES—SALT RIVER	Etching	George Elbert Burr	137
"ELEPHANT'S FEET"—NEAR RED LAKE, ARIZONA	Photograph	Josef Muench	138

LIST OF ILLUSTRATIONS

Navajo Sheep in Monument Valley	Photograph	Chuck Abbott	138
Light Snows in Utah	Photograph	Lee for F.S.A.	139
Fertile Valley—San Cristobal, N.M.	Photograph	Lee for F.S.A.	139
Cactus Country	Photograph	Chuck Abbott	140
Yucca and Wildflowers	Photograph	Chuck Abbott	141
Desert Nocturne	Photograph	Josef Muench	141
Bright Angel Point—Grand Canyon	Photograph	Hubert A. Lowman	142
The Grand Canyon	Photograph	U.S. Department of the Interior	143
Dead Wood—Grand Canyon	Photograph	Cedric Wright	143
The Bright Angel Trail—Grand Canyon	Lithograph	Joseph Pennell	144
South Rim of the Grand Canyon	Photograph	Laura Gilpin	145
Early Morning in the Grand Canyon	Photograph	Ernest Knee	145
Mitchell Pass—Scotts Bluff National Monument	Photograph	Geo. A. Grant for U.S. Dept. of the Interior	146
Bryce Canyon	Photograph	Laura Gilpin	146
Desert Sycamore	Photograph	Esther Henderson	147
Santa Anita Pass	Etching	R. Stephens Wright	148
Logging Camp in Oregon	Photograph	Lee for F.S.A.	148
Elk Hunters	Etching	Levon West	149
Coastal Pastures—California	Photograph	Grant Duggins	149
Death Valley Dunes—California	Photograph	Geo. A. Grant for U.S. Dept. of the Interior	150
Death Valley—California	Photograph	Grant Duggins	150
Storm on East Escapement—Sierra Nevada	Photograph	Cedric Wright	151
Grande Ronde Valley—Oregon	Photograph	Minor White	152
Sky Pastures	Photograph	Roi Partridge	152

OUR ARCHITECTURAL INHERITANCE

The Library—University of Virginia	Photograph	Samuel Chamberlain	153
Springtime in Salem	Drypoint	Samuel Chamberlain	154
Weathered Clapboards	Photograph	Samuel Chamberlain	154
Church on the Green—Middlebury, Vt.	Photograph	Samuel Chamberlain	155
The Parson Capen House, Topsfield, Mass.	Photograph	Samuel Chamberlain	156
Longfellow's Wayside Inn, South Sudbury, Mass.	Photograph	Samuel Chamberlain	157
Bulfinch Hall—Andover, Mass.	Photograph	Samuel Chamberlain	157
Old Buildings in the Harvard Yard, Cambridge, Mass.	Photograph	Samuel Chamberlain	158

THE STATE HOUSE—BOSTON, MASS.	Photograph	Samuel Chamberlain	158
INDEPENDENCE HALL—PHILADELPHIA, PA.	Photograph	Ewing Galloway	159
THE CAPITOL DOME, WASHINGTON, D.C.	Photograph	Ewing Galloway	160
MOUNT VERNON	Photograph	Frances Benjamin Johnston	161
THE WHITE HOUSE	Photograph	Delano for F.S.A.	161
THE APOTHECARY'S SHOP, WILLIAMSBURG, VIRGINIA	Drypoint	Samuel Chamberlain	162
MONTICELLO—NEAR CHARLOTTESVILLE, VIRGINIA	Photograph	Samuel Chamberlain	163
THE CAPITOL—WILLIAMSBURG, VA.	Drypoint	Samuel Chamberlain	163
SPRINGTIME IN WILLIAMSBURG	Photograph	Richard Garrison	164
OTWELL—MARYLAND	Photograph	Frances Benjamin Johnston	165
SWEET HALL—VIRGINIA	Photograph	Frances Benjamin Johnston	165
BLACKLOCK HOUSE—CHARLESTON, S.C.	Photograph	Frances Benjamin Johnston	166
CHURCH STREET—CHARLESTON, S.C.	Photograph	Frances Benjamin Johnston	167
RUINS OF SHELDON CHURCH—S.C.	Photograph	Frances Benjamin Johnston	167
GENERAL BRAGG'S HOUSE—MOBILE, ALA.	Photograph	Frances Benjamin Johnston	168
PAST GLORY—BELLEGROVE, LA.	Photograph	Frances Benjamin Johnston	168
UPSON HOUSE—ATHENS, GEORGIA	Photograph	Frances Benjamin Johnston	169
BELLE HELENA PLANTATION—LA.	Photograph	Vories Fisher	170
GREENWOOD PLANTATION—LOUISIANA	Photograph	Frances Benjamin Johnston	170
THE HERMITAGE—PLANTATION IN LOUISIANA	Photograph	Vories Fisher	171
COURTYARD IN THE VIEUX CARRÉ, NEW ORLEANS	Photograph	Frances Benjamin Johnston	171
THE OLD STATE CAPITOL, DES MOINES, IOWA	Photograph	Ewing Galloway	172
THE CONCEPTION MISSION—NEAR SAN ANTONIO, TEXAS	Photograph	Underwood-Stratton	172
MISSION SAN JOSE—SAN ANTONIO	Photograph	Claude B. Aniol	173
THE ALAMO—SAN ANTONIO	Photograph	Claude B. Aniol	173
TUMACACORI MISSION—ARIZONA	Photograph	Hubert A. Lowman	174
OLD SPANISH MISSION, TAOS, NEW MEXICO	Photograph	Rothstein for F.S.A.	174
MISSION SAN XAVIER—ARIZONA	Photograph	Josef Muench	175
MISSION SAN XAVIER—ARIZONA	Photograph	Esther Henderson	175
FAR WEST ARCHITECTURE, VIRGINIA CITY, NEVADA	Photograph	Rothstein for F.S.A.	176
OLD COURTHOUSE—TOMBSTONE, ARIZONA	Photograph	Chuck Abbott	176
SAN JUAN BAUTISTA MISSION—CALIFORNIA	Photograph	Will Connell	177
SANTA BARBARA MISSION	Photograph	Will Connell	177
SANTA YNEZ MISSION—CALIFORNIA	Photograph	Grant Duggins	178
SAN LUIS REY MISSION	Photograph	Grant Duggins	178

MOUNTAIN RANGES AND THE NATION'S PARKS

YOSEMITE FALLS	Photograph	Padilla Studios	179
ESTES PARK—COLORADO	Photograph	Tet Borsig	180
PIKE'S PEAK BEYOND A SCREEN OF SAPLINGS	Photograph	Laura Gilpin	180
MT. CANNON—MONTANA	Photograph	Hileman for Glacier National Park	181
THE MOUNTAINS IN WHITE	Photograph	Fritz Kaeser	182
THE MOUNTAINS IN BLACK—WEST GATE	Etching	Levon West	182
WINTRY SILHOUETTE	Photograph	Josef Muench	183
GOAT MOUNTAIN—MONTANA	Photograph	Hileman for Glacier National Park	184
THE PEAK	Etching	Levon West	184
THE MISSION RANGE—MONTANA	Photograph	U.S. Forest Service	185
THE BAD LANDS—SOUTH DAKOTA	Photograph	Ewing Galloway	185
WALLOWA MOUNTAINS—OREGON	Photograph	Minor White	186
CARSON PASS—CALIFORNIA	Photograph	McCurry	186
SAN FRANCISCO PEAKS—ARIZONA	Photograph	Esther Henderson	187
THE SIERRAS IN MIDWINTER	Photograph	Josef Muench	188
MOUNT SHASTA	Photograph	Ray Atkeson	188
MOUNT HOOD	Photograph	Ray Atkeson	189
SHUKSAN IN WINTER	Etching	Helen A. Loggie	189
MOUNT HOOD	Photograph	Ray Atkeson	190
THE CASCADE RANGE—WASHINGTON	Photograph	Ray Atkeson	190
TRAIL APPROACHING MOUNT WHITNEY	Photograph	Cedric Wright	191
SUNSET FROM MUIR PASS—CALIFORNIA	Photograph	Cedric Wright	191
PEAK OF MOUNT HOOD IN THE CLOUDS	Photograph	Ray Atkeson	192
MIDWINTER ON MOUNT HOOD	Photograph	Ray Atkeson	192
DRIFT SNOW	Photograph	Josef Muench	193
REFLECTIONS IN THE HIGH SIERRA	Photograph	Josef Muench	193
AUTUMN SNOW ON MOUNT ADAMS	Photograph	Ray Atkeson	194
ALPINE MEADOWS—MOUNT RAINIER	Photograph	U.S. Dept. of the Interior	194
DEADWOOD DRAMA—MOUNT RAINIER	Photograph	U.S. Dept. of the Interior	195
THE GATES OF YOSEMITE VALLEY	Photograph	Ansel Adams for U.S. Dept. of the Interior	196
YOSEMITE VALLEY AFTER A SNOW STORM	Photograph	Ralph Anderson for U.S. Dept. of the Interior	196
SEQUOIAS IN THE SNOW	Photograph	Ralph Anderson for U.S. Dept. of the Interior	197
EL CAPITAN—YOSEMITE VALLEY	Photograph	U.S. Dept. of the Interior	198
HORSE RIDGE—YOSEMITE NATIONAL PARK	Photograph	U.S. Dept. of the Interior	199

HALF DOME—YOSEMITE NATIONAL PARK	Photograph	Padilla Studios for U.S. Dept. of the Interior	199
GUNSIGHT LAKE	Photograph	Hileman for Glacier Naitonal Park	200
TEMPLE OF TINAWANA—ZION NATIONAL PARK	Photograph	Geo. A. Grant for U.S. Dept. of the Interior	200
GRINNELL GLACIER	Photograph	Hileman for Glacier National Park	201
GLACIER LILLIES—MOUNT CLEMENTS	Photograph	Hileman for Glacier National Park	201
BEAR GRASS—MOUNT GOULD	Photograph	Hileman for Glacier National Park	202
BADGER PASS IN WINTER—YOSEMITE	Photograph	Ansel Adams for U.S. Dept. of the Interior	202
MOUNTAIN HIGHWAY	Photograph	Hileman for Glacier National Park	203
BLUE POOLS ON JUPITER TERRACE, YELLOWSTONE NATIONAL PARK	Photograph	Ray Atkeson	203
THE MONARCHS—SEQUOIA NATIONAL PARK	Photograph	U.S. Dept. of the Interior	204
FOREST GIANTS	Photograph	Gabriel Moulin for U.S. Dept. of the Interior	205
SUNBURST	Photograph	Ray Atkeson	206

THE SEACOASTS

CAPE ELIZABETH—MAINE	Photograph	Ewing Galloway	207
SMOKE HOUSES—THOMASTON, MAINE	Photograph	Samuel Chamberlain	208
PORTLAND HEAD LIGHT—MAINE	Photograph	Ewing Galloway	208
LOBSTERMAN'S COVE	Lithograph	Stow Wengenroth	209
AFTER THE RAIN	Lithograph	Stow Wengenroth	209
SEINE BOATS—GLOUCESTER, MASS.	Photograph	Samuel Chamberlain	210
ROCKY NECK—GLOUCESTER	Etching	Max Kuehn	210
THE OLD WHALER "CHARLES W. MORGAN"	Photograph	Samuel Chamberlain	211
BOATS AT DAWN	Etching	Frank W. Benson	211
THE CLIFFS OF GAY HEAD—MARTHA'S VINEYARD, MASS.	Photograph	Samuel Chamberlain	212
THE GUNNER'S BLIND	Etching	Frank W. Benson	212
RACE WEEK, MARBLEHEAD, MASS.	Photograph	Samuel Chamberlain	213
PORTSMOUTH HARBOR—NEW HAMPSHIRE	Etching	Charles H. Woodbury	213
STONINGTON SUNSET—CONNECTICUT	Drypoint	Samuel Chamberlain	214
COAST STORM	Etching	C. Jac Young	214
COMING IN	Etching	C. Jac Young	215

LIST OF ILLUSTRATIONS

"Motif No. 1"—Rockport, Mass.	Photograph	Gerhard H. Bakker	215
Black Squall	Photograph	Eleanor Park Custis	216
Seine Fishermen	Photograph	Eleanor Park Custis	217
The Dunes—Montauk Point, L.I.	Photograph	Tet Borsig	218
Net Pattern—Long Island	Photograph	Tet Borsig	218
Reflections in Boston Harbor	Photograph	Frank R. Fraprie	219
The Shore at Montauk Point, L.I.	Photograph	Tet Borsig	220
Oyster Boats—Cape Cod	Photograph	Ralph E. Day	221
Lower Manhattan Seen by the Camera	Photograph	Ewing Galloway	222
Lower Manhattan Seen by the Lithographer	Lithograph	Joseph Pennell	222
The Queen and Her Slaves	Etching	Otto Kuhler	223
Civic Insomnia	Aquatint	Gerald K. Geerlings	223
The Spires of Manhattan	Etching	Otto Kuhler	224
New York Harbor	Photograph	Tet Borsig	224
Delaware Fishing Village	Photograph	Vachon for F.S.A.	225
Oyster Boats in Deal's Island Bay	Photograph	Delano for F.S.A.	225
Shores of Maryland	Softground Etching	F. Townsend Morgan	226
Fishing Fleet—Hampton, Virginia	Photograph	Samuel Chamberlain	226
Windswept	Etching	Alfred Hutty	227
Sand Dunes—St. Augustine, Florida	Photograph	Arthur Hammond	228
Beach Grass—Florida	Photograph	Arthur Hammond	228
The Breakers	Photograph	Ray Atkeson	229
Wings Against the Sky—Mississippi	Photograph	Anthony V. Ragusin	230
The Oyster Fleet—Biloxi, Miss.	Photograph	Anthony V. Ragusin	230
Florida Shore	Photograph	Arthur Hammond	231
Pacific Sands	Photograph	Brett Weston	232
California Surf	Photograph	Robert Ingram	232
Fish Harbor	Etching	R. Stephens Wright	233
Snug Harbor	Etching	Armin Hanson	233
Small Mission Wharf	Etching	John W. Winkler	234
View from Telegraph Hill—San Francisco	Etching	John W. Winkler	234
Fishermen's Wharf—San Francisco	Photograph	Robert Ingram	235
Puget Sound—Washington	Etching	R. Stephens Wright	236
Venice in Oakland	Photograph	Roi Partridge	236
Composition at Low Tide	Photograph	Roi Partridge	237
Arch Cape—Oregon	Photograph	Ray Atkeson	238
Cape Kiwanda—Oregon	Photograph	Ray Atkeson	239
Cannon Beach—Oregon	Photograph	Ray Atkeson	239
The Pacific	Photograph	Roi Partridge	240
Stone Barn	Wood Engraving	Thomas W. Nason	241